I0814536

Amazing Young People

SACAGAWEA

Martha London

DiscoverRoo
An Imprint of Pop!
popbooksonline.com

abdobooks.com

Published by Pop!, a division of ABDO, PO Box 398166, Minneapolis, Minnesota 55439.

Printed in the United States of America, North Mankato, Minnesota

052019
092019

THIS BOOK CONTAINS RECYCLED MATERIALS

Cover Photo: Kevin E. Schmidt/Quad-City Times/Zuma Wire/Alamy

Interior Photos: Kevin E. Schmidt/Quad-City Times/Zuma Wire/Alamy, 1; Historic Images/Alamy, 5; Shutterstock Images, 6 (left), 6 (right), 15, 22 (left), 23 (bottom), 25, 28, 30 (right), 31; Photo Researchers/Science History Images/Alamy, 7; Red Line Editorial, 8; iStockphoto, 9, 12, 18, 26, 30 (left); Library of Congress, 11; Pictures Now/Alamy, 13, 19; Album/Florilegius/Newscom, 14; Angel Wynn/Danita Delimont/Alamy, 17; Granger Historical Picture Archive, 20–21; Charlie Riedel/AP Images, 22 (right); North Wind Picture Archives, 23 (top), 27; Tom Bauer/Missoulian/AP Images, 29

Editor: Brienna Rossiter
Series Designer: Sarah Taplin

Library of Congress Control Number: 2018964789

Publisher's Cataloging-in-Publication Data

Names: London, Martha, author.

Title: Sacagawea / by Martha London.

Description: Minneapolis, Minnesota : Pop!, 2020 | Series: Amazing young people | Includes online resources and index.

Identifiers: ISBN 9781532163708 (lib. bdg.) | ISBN 9781644940433 (pbk.) | ISBN 9781532165146 (ebook)

Subjects: LCSH: Sacagawea--Juvenile literature. | Lewis and Clark Expedition (1804-1806)--Juvenile literature. | Shoshone women--Biography--Juvenile literature. | Shoshoni Indians--Biography--Juvenile literature.

Classification: DDC 978.0049 [B]--dc23

WELCOME TO DiscoverRoo!

Pop open this book and you'll find QR codes loaded with information, so you can learn even more!

Scan this code* and others like it while you read, or visit the website below to make this book pop!

popbooksonline.com/sacagawea

*Scanning QR codes requires a web-enabled smart device with a QR code reader app and a camera.

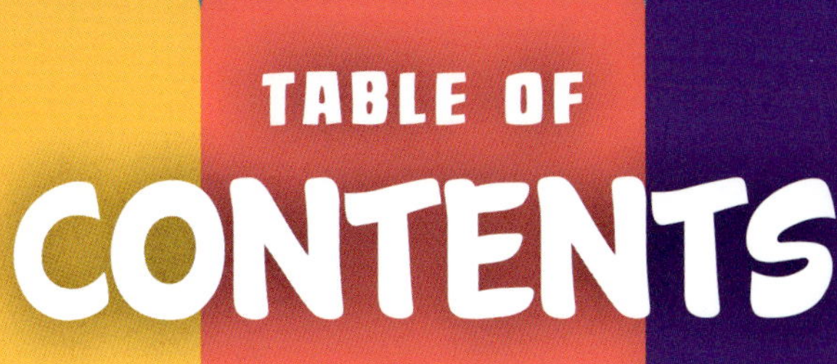

TABLE OF CONTENTS

Sacagawea was a Shoshone woman. She was part of the Lewis and Clark **Expedition**. Its members explored North America from 1804 to 1806. They traveled west of the Mississippi River.

Sacagawea was the only woman who traveled with the expedition.

Meriwether Lewis (left) and William Clark became friends while serving in the US Army.

In 1803, the United States bought a huge area of land from France. US leaders wanted to learn about the land and the people who lived there. They

sent a group of men to explore it. Meriwether Lewis and William Clark led the group.

THE LEWIS AND CLARK EXPEDITION

The expedition began near St. Louis, Missouri. The men planned to go all the way to the Pacific Ocean and back. At first, they traveled in boats along the Missouri River. Later they rode horses. During the journey, they drew maps. They also recorded the plants and animals they saw.

Clark drew this map of the Pacific coast.

THE LEWIS AND CLARK EXPEDITION

Sacagawea was an **interpreter** for the explorers during part of the journey. She helped them talk with American Indians they met along the way. She also helped them get food and other important supplies.

DID YOU KNOW?

Sacagawea traveled with the expedition for more than 4,000 miles.

CHAPTER 2

EARLY LIFE

Sacagawea was born sometime around 1788. She was part of the Shoshone tribe. Members of the Hidatsa tribe captured her when she was 12 years old. They took her far from home.

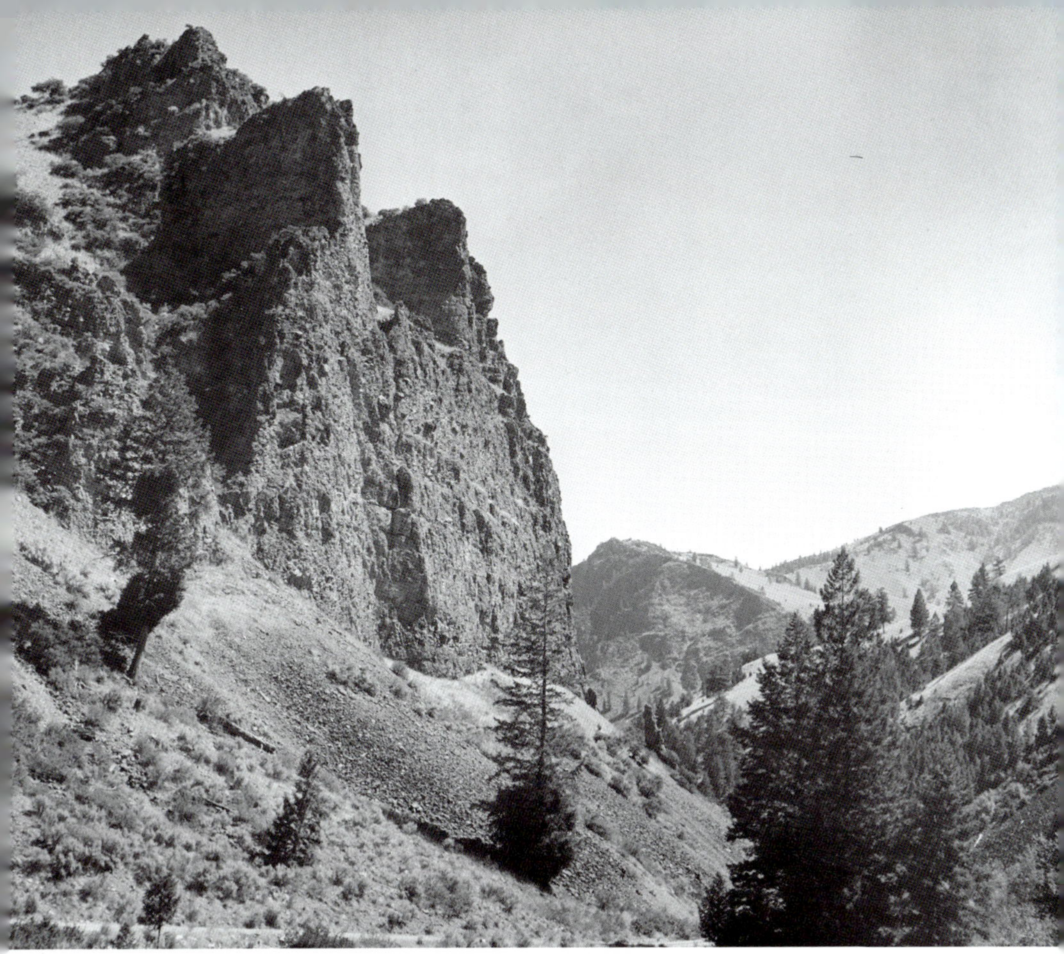

Sacagawea was born in Lemhi County, an area that is now part of the state of Idaho.

The name Sacagawea means "bird woman" in the Hidatsa language.

Fur traders often lived and traded with American Indian tribes.

A French **fur trader** forced Sacagawea to be his wife. His name was Toussaint Charbonneau. He and Sacagawea lived in a Hidatsa village.

It was located in what is now North Dakota. Lewis and Clark reached this area in the fall of 1804. They built **Fort Mandan** to stay the winter. They also hired the couple as **interpreters**.

Hidatsa villages had dome-shaped homes.

An illustration from 1841 shows the clothing a Hidatsa woman might have worn.

Sacagawea knew the languages of the Hidatsa and Shoshone tribes. Charbonneau could speak Hidatsa and

French. They could work together to speak with American Indian tribes. They helped the explorers trade with the tribes for food and supplies.

DID YOU KNOW?

Neither Sacagawea nor Charbonneau spoke English. Another man translated their answers for Lewis and Clark.

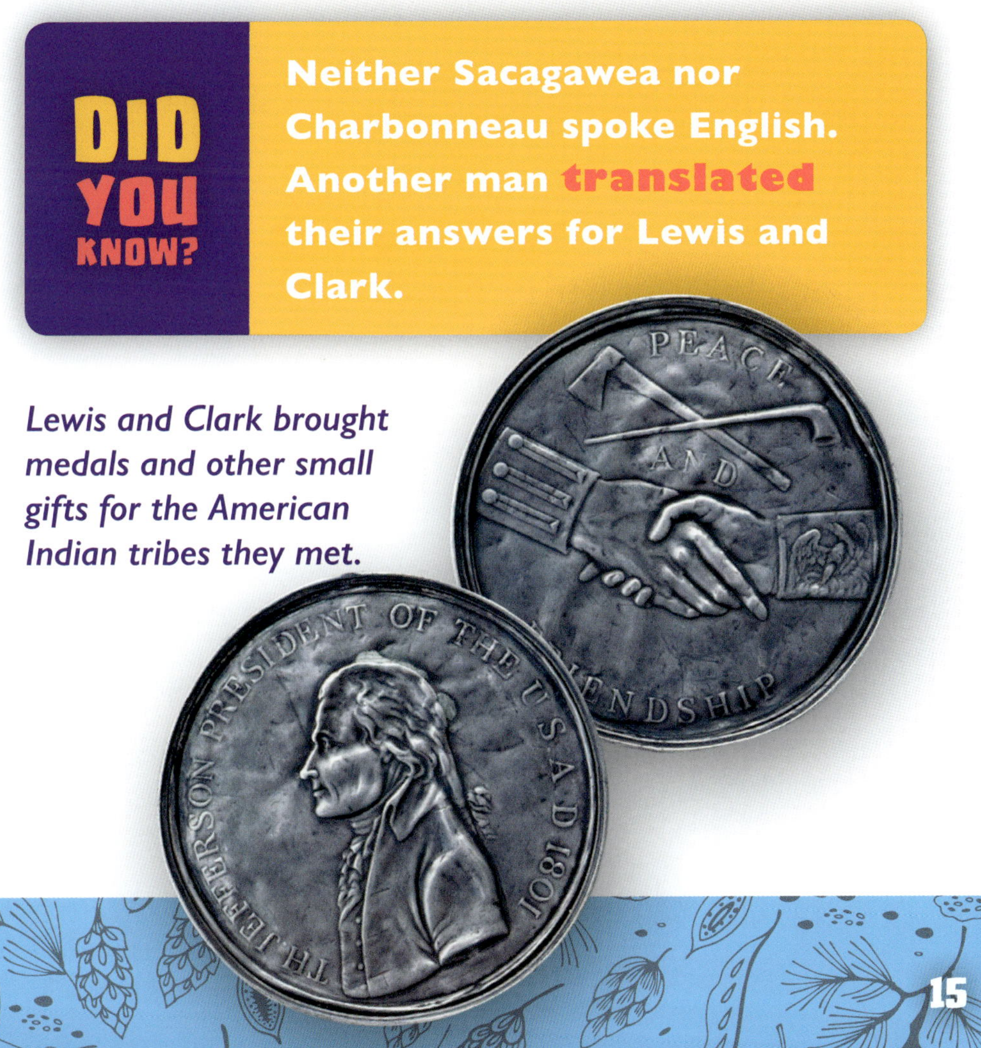

Lewis and Clark brought medals and other small gifts for the American Indian tribes they met.

CHAPTER 3

THE EXPEDITION

The **expedition** left the Hidatsa village in April 1805. Sacagawea was a teenager. She brought her two-month-old son. His name was Jean Baptiste. Their presence helped show that the expedition was

COMPLETE AN ACTIVITY HERE!

Sacagawea placed her son in a cradleboard so she could carry him on her back as they traveled.

peaceful. Groups wouldn't bring women or children if they planned to attack.

The explorers used dugout canoes for part of their journey.

In August, the explorers reached the Rocky Mountains. Their boats could go no farther. Sacagawea helped them get

Sacagawea recognized some landmarks from when she was a young girl.

horses from the Shoshone tribe. She also helped them find a guide. The guide led them across the mountains.

Sacagawea's brother was the Shoshone tribe's leader. She had not seen him for many years.

Crossing the mountains was very hard. The explorers faced rough ground and cold weather. They nearly starved.

The explorers struggled through deep snow as they crossed the Rocky Mountains.

But the Nez Perce tribe helped them. In November 1805, the expedition finally reached the Pacific Ocean.

TIMELINE

1788

Sacagawea is born into a Shoshone tribe around this time.

1800

Sacagawea is kidnapped by members of the Hidatsa tribe.

1804

The Lewis and Clark Expedition begins traveling west from Missouri.

1806

Sacagawea and Charbonneau return to the Hidatsa village.

1805

Sacagawea and Charbonneau join the expedition.

1812

Sacagawea dies in December.

CHAPTER 4

A LASTING IMPACT

The explorers built a **fort** and stayed there during the winter. In March 1806, they began the long journey home. By August, they reached the Hidatsa village. Sacagawea and her family stayed there.

LEARN MORE HERE!

The explorers stayed in Fort Clatsop from December 1805 to March 1806.

The rest of the group continued east.

They traveled back toward St. Louis.

Sacagawea collected edible roots and berries.

Charbonneau received $500 and 320 **acres** of land for his work as an **interpreter**. Sacagawea had

translated too. She also cooked, mended clothes, and gathered plants to eat. But she was not paid.

Lewis and Clark described Sacagawea's work in their journals.

Statues of Sacagawea stand along the expedition's route.

Little is known about the rest of Sacagawea's life. She had a daughter sometime after 1810. And she likely died in 1812. Today, Sacagawea is remembered for her important role in the Lewis and Clark **Expedition**. In fact, some historians doubt it would have succeeded without her.

DID YOU KNOW?

During the expedition, Clark and Sacagawea became friends. He took care of her children after she died.

Modern actors ride along the trail the expedition followed.

MAKING CONNECTIONS

TEXT-TO-SELF

Sacagawea traveled with the Lewis and Clark Expedition for thousands of miles. What is the longest trip you have ever taken?

TEXT-TO-TEXT

Have you read other books about women who were part of important events in US history? Who were they, and what did they do?

TEXT-TO-WORLD

The Lewis and Clark Expedition traveled west of the Mississippi River. What places are people mapping or exploring today?

GLOSSARY

acre – a measurement of land.

expedition – a group of people exploring a new place.

fort – a strong building or group of buildings, especially one made for people to live in or to defend against attack.

fur trader – a person who buys and sells animal fur.

interpreter – someone who speaks multiple languages to help groups of people talk to each other.

translate – to take a word or sentence in one language and say it in another so a person can understand.

INDEX

ONLINE RESOURCES

popbooksonline.com

Scan this code* and others like it while you read, or visit the website below to make this book pop!

popbooksonline.com/sacagawea

*Scanning QR codes requires a web-enabled smart device with a QR code reader app and a camera.